☆ # 100 ☆

FAMOUS
COCKTAILS

100

FAMOUS COCKTAILS

THE
ROMANCE OF WINES AND LIQUORS
ETIQUETTE . . . . RECIPES

PUBLISHED IN COLLABORATION WITH

Oscar of The Waldorf

DECORATIONS BY HENRY STAHLHUT

Copyright © 1934 by Kenilworth Press, Inc.
This edition copyright © 2023 by Commonwealth Book Company. Inc.

All rights reserved. No part of this book may be reproduced in any form or by any means without the prior written consent of the publisher, excepting brief quotes used in reviews.
Printed in the United States of America.

ISBN: 978-1-948986-71-7

TABLE OF CONTENTS

Romance of Wines and Liquors..................................Pages 6 to 11
The Correct Service (Proper Foods—the Right Temperature)........Pages 12 to 15
Correct Glassware..Pages 16 to 19
Waldorf Bar History..Pages 20 to 21
Drinks Made Famous at the Waldorf................................Pages 22 to 45

COCKTAILS

Absinthe	23	Martini Dry	28
Adonis	23	Mae West	29
Alexander	23	Merry Widow	29
Astoria	23	Monopole	29
Bacardi Cocktail	23	New Waldorf	29
Bijou	24	Old Fashioned	29
Bird	24	Orange Blossom	30
Blue Moon	24	Peacock Alley	30
Brandy	24	Peacock Gallery	30
Bridal	24	Peg O' My Heart	30
Bronx	25	Pick Me Up	30
Champagne	25	Poet's Dream	31
Charlie Chaplin	25	Rob Roy	31
Clover Club	25	Russian Grand Duke	31
Clover Leaf	25	Salome	31
Creole	26	September Morn	31
Daiquiri	26	Sherry-Netherland	31
Dubonnet	26	Side Car	32
Full House	26	Sloe Gin	32
Gin	26	Soul Kiss	32
Goat's Delight	27	Sours	32
Good Times	27	Toddies	32
Happy Days	27	Tom Gin	32
Honolulu	27	Trilby	33
Hop Frog	27	Waldorf	33
Jack Rose	28	Waldorf Gloom Lifter	33
Manhattan	28	Waldorf-Astoria	33
Martell	28	Whiskey Sour	33
Martini	28	Zaza	33

HIGHBALLS BALLS AND FANCY DRINKS

Baby Titty	34	John Collins	39
Brandy and Ginger Ale Frappe	34	Lalla Rookh	39
Brandy Fizz	34	Mint Cooler	39
Brandy Float	34	Mint Julep	40
Brandy Julep	34	Morning Glory Fizz	40
Brandy Punch	34	New Orleans Fizz	40
Brandy Smash	35	Orange Cognac	40
Brandy Toddy	35	Pousse Cafe Waldorf	40
Champagne Cup	35	Remsen Cooler	41
Champagne Punch	35	Rickeys	41
Claret Cup Waldorf	36	Roosevelt Punch	41
Claret Lemonade	36	Royal Fizz	41
Claret Punch	36	Sherry Cobler	41
Egg Noggs	36	Silver Fizz	42
Fascination	37	Sloe Gin Fizz	42
Fish House Punch	37	Snowball	42
Flips	37	Starlight Roof Garden Cooler	42
Floradora Sextette	37	Tom and Jerry	42
Gin Buck	37	Tom Collins	43
Gin Daisy	38	Waldorf Fizz	43
Gin Fizz	38	Whiskey and Mint	43
Golden Fizz	38	Whiskey Daisy	43
Golden West	38	Whiskey Fizz	44
Grenadine Fizz	38	Whiskey Mint Julep	44
Highballs	39	Whiskey Punch	44
Honeymoon	39	Whiskey Smash	44
Horses Neck	39		

CORDIALS

Angel's Blush or Kiss	45	Brandy Scaffa	45
Angel's Dream	45	Come Up—Sometime	45

THE ROMANCE OF

WINES AND LIQUORS

WHEN mankind ascended from savagery and developed civilized refinements the right use of wines and other alcoholic beverages became an art, and an encouragement to all the arts. No nation, past or present, ever produced great music or sculpture, painting or literature, on an unrelieved diet of plain water! The great peoples of the earth—notwithstanding certain "reforming" elements to whom these spiritual values mean little—have taken the products of a beneficent soil, fermented or distilled them, and quenched their thirst with cheerful thanks to the gods for such blessings.

Consequently the art of right drinking is to a degree, the story of the human race. The ancient Hebrews, migrating into the Holy Land, dreamed of the day when every man should contentedly drink of his own vine beneath his own fig tree, in those times the criterion of prosperity. The Greeks of the classic Golden Age, leaving to posterity their priceless legacies of the Iliad and the Parthenon, of Socrates, Aristophanes and Pythagoras, cultivated the grape even on the slopes of high Olympus, at whose summit Bacchus and his fellow deities quaffed goblets of nectar at fair Hebe's hands.

The Romans, organizers of law and statecraft and world unity, encouraged the making of good wine throughout their tremendous empire. The sturdy English yeomen of Crecy and Agincourt were fortified by good Saxon ale as well as the wines of the continent. Our Puritan forebears, laying the political and moral foundations of a new world, thought it not ungodly to imbibe rum and other ardent spirits. Even the founder of Christianity commanded that those common foods, bread and wine, be used in the reverent act of worship bequeathed to his followers, and St. Paul the Apostle advised "a little wine for thy stomach's sake." Where is civilization to be found without good beverages?

Men and women lovingly cultivate the grape on the gentle, sunny slopes of the Rhone, on the terraced banks of the picturesque Moselle, in Italy, Spain, Hungary, Portugal—in every place where sun and soil and climate lend their aid. From century to century they tend the vines, gather ripe fruit, extract its life blood, age it, blend it, making glad the hearts of their fellow-creatures while earning the bread of their own children. It is no coincidence that these people are among the happiest in the world. Would you have quiet romance in your heart? Go to the terraced vineyards where generation after generation cultivates the grape. Do you seek genuine merriment? Visit the harvest wine festivals, and while delighting your palate fail not to feast your eyes on the loveliness of those ancient countrysides.

The greatest wine country is, of course, France, whence come the numerous vintages of Bordeaux and of Burgundy, both white and red; of Champagne, home of the world's favorite sparkling wines; of many clarets often imitated, the sincerest form of flattery, and such regional wines as those of Anjou, still or sparkling. Our best known German wines are those of the Rhine terraces and the light but not thin beverages of the Moselle. One of the world's finest types of wine, Sherry, is Spanish, blended from the grapes of several vineyards. Tokay, at its best "the wine of kings," is a rich Hungarian fluid, and the sweet wines of Madeira and the Canaries are noted in literature— as in Sir Walter Scott's "Ivanhoe."

Port is a product of Portugal, and like Sherry is a blend. This wine, which has been imitated with some success in California and other suitable regions, is not always understood. "Vintage" Port is very fruity and full-bodied, and real connoisseurs serve it with pride, while "tawny" and "ruby" Ports are generally lighter though by no means to be despised. The term full-bodied, incidentally, connotes other qualities besides mere alcoholic content. Almost all wines are obtainable in many varieties and grades, some sweeter, some more dry: some heavier, others lighter, and from very fine to comparatively poor. The word "Chateau" when truthfully used on a French label, indicates maturing and bottling by the owners of the vineyard where the grapes were grown.

The buying of wine is as great an art as its wise use, for important reasons. In any grape region the yield of one year may be excellent and in another relatively poor, and once in a decade it may be of such extraordinary quality as to command an extraordinary price. Individual tastes must also be considered, as well as the reputation of the wine-maker. The average man cannot be expected to know the innumerable details in this subject, but must deal with a reliable house in which he can trust, whose trained buyers are equipped to select properly labeled goods at the right prices. Some American wines, for instance, are less expensive than imported ones and yet of enough merit to deserve respect, for in such parts of the United States as California a particular grape may find hospitality in a certain kind of soil. But the maturing and blending of wine is not done overnight, and the customer is actually in the hands of his dealer.

A few words about other beverages may be interesting.

Many a connoisseur of brandy, if asked about its origin, would be caught uninformed. It is simply a wine or blend of wines, distilled into a liquor of higher alcoholic content. A French authority states that there are but eight standard brandies, the best known of which is probably Cognac, named from a town on the River Charente in France.

Another ardent spirit, rum, is distilled from molasses or cane sugar. Perhaps the most appreciated brand known to Americans is Bacardi, produced in Cuba. By the way, who does not remember when "rum" was the generic term for all alcoholic beverages in certain quarters, and Demon Rum shared with John Barleycorn the blame for all evil? But then if sinners drank it so did many a saint!

Scotch and Irish whiskeys are distilled by different process from barley; genuine Scotch is made only in Scotland, its taste being partly derived from the peat fires used in manufacture. Bourbon is an American distillate of corn or maize; and rye whiskey, beloved by many for ginger-ale highballs, explains itself. In all these whiskeys other grains are added to impart the correct flavor. Gin, used as a base in most cocktails—and fearfully imitated during the late sad era—is also distilled from grain, with an aromatic flavor added. There are many national distillates also, such as absinthe in France and Vodka in Russia.

Among the cordials or "liqueurs"—heavy, syrupy liquids best suited to the close of a good dinner—we have the light amber-tinted Strega from Italy; Cointreau, known to the American doughboy as Triple Sec, is a French cordial clear as water. The most famous of the liqueurs tell highly romantic tales—Benedictine and Chartreuse were both invented and manufactured by busy monks. The former was created by Dom Bernardo Vincelli of the Benedictine Abbey of Fécamp, a religious house founded in the year 665, and its "D.O.M." on labels of the genuine, representing the Latin phrase *Deo optimo maximo*, is a reverent ascription of praise by the monks who produced this wonderful beverage under a secret formula until their community was dissolved in the last century.

Chartreuse, its green and yellow rival, was also produced by clergymen, being perfected by a clever brother of the Carthusian order about 1757. But space forbids the detailed story of many beverages. It may only be added that Champagne, as we know it, was also the discovery of a monk—Dom Perignon, the genial Father Cellarer of the Abbey of Hanvillers about two and one-half centuries ago.

THE CORRECT

SERVICE

The term "correct service" has a double meaning. In the first place, long experience has universally shown that certain kinds of beverages are best with certain kinds of foods, for stomach and palate alike. This still leaves a considerable variety of choice to the gourmet. The second meaning follows: it is socially correct to serve beverages according to the common experience in health and taste.

Etiquette is always a matter of genuine consideration for others. Should a guest dislike cocktails before dinner one will serve him another drink if possible; dry sherry will make a perfect appetizer. Incidentally, it is served in a sherry glass, not a cocktail glass.

The general rules are very simple—white wines are served with fish and, as a rule, red wines with meat. Some prefer a single beverage such as champagne throughout the meal. White wines are cooled in the refrigerator, red wines are served at room temperature, and sparkling wines are served as cold as possible. The following pages contain detailed suggestions approved by the world-famous "host," Oscar of the Waldorf.

VERY DRY WHITE BURGUNDY
Chablis, Charmes, Meursault, Pouilly
At cold cave temperature

> *With oysters, clams, lobster, etc. (grilled or cold); fish and sea-foods generally; eggs, galantine, cold ham.*

PARTLY DRY WHITE WINES
Burgundy: Goutte d'Or, Montrachet
Bordeaux: Graves, Sauternes, Barsac
Cold, or slightly iced

> *With sweetbreads, patties, paté de foie gras; lobster Newburg, sole Normande, well-seasoned fish generally; chicken or ham with spiced sauces.*

LIGHT RED WINES (CLARETS)
Lafite, Latour, Haut-Brion, Ausone, Rauzan. Also Chateauneuf and Hermitage.
Room temperature

> *With roast duck, chicken, turkey, pigeon, quail, pheasant; veal, roast or chops; lamb, roast or broiled; small game, such as grouse and partridge; with cheese courses.*

HEAVY RED WINES OF BURGUNDY

Chambertin, Corton, Beaune, Volnay, Pommard

Room temperature

> With beef, steak or roast; mutton; wild duck; goose, rabbit, and venison; any wild game. Also with cheese.

HEAVY WHITE BORDEAUX OR ANJOU

Chateaux Yquem, Clemens, Guiraud, Vigneau

Chateau Montcontour, Quarts de Chaume

Very cold, or cold cave temperature

> With Bouillabaise, sweetbreads, lobster Armoricaine, poularde; also with desserts, fruits, etc.

CHAMPAGNES

Heidsieck & Co. Dry Monopole

Pol Roger, Veuve Clicquot, Pommery,

Mumm, Heidsieck, Roederer, Ayala

Thoroughly iced

> With any or all courses as desired; for after-dinner speeches and toasts, and festive occasions.

CORRECT GLASSWARE

Wines

Sherry   Sauternes*   Hock or Rhine Wine

Pale Green or Light Amber Glass

Port   Still Burgundy   Claret**   Hollow-stemmed Burgundy for sparkling wine only

*Sauternes a slighted tinted glass (green or pink)
**Claret glasses should always be clear crystal

Cocktails

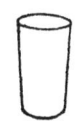 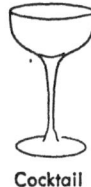 

Delmonico   Cocktail   Old Fashioned

Champagne

Goblet Champagne

Saucer Champagne

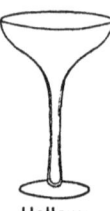
Hollow-stemmed Champagne

Optional use of any glasses above

Whiskey

1½ oz. Whiskey or Bar Glass

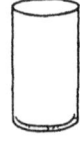
8 oz. Highball Glass

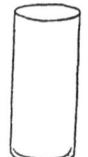
12 oz. Highball Glass

Special Glasses

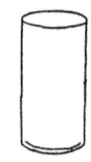
10 oz. Fizz or Lemonade Glass

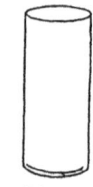
14 oz. Tom Collins Glass

Cordials

Liqueurs

Brandy
Pony

Creme De Menthe
Frappé

Brandy (Tulip
Shaped) Snifter
Large

Brandy (Tulip
Shaped) Snifter
Small

Beer

Pilsner

Hollow Stem

Goblet

Beer Mug

WALDORF BAR HISTORY
OLD AND NEW

THE old Waldorf-Astoria, razed a few years ago to make way for the Empire State Building, was unquestionably the most famous hostelry in the United States, possibly in the entire world. Visiting royalty, wearers of coronets, diplomatists and other persons of distinction from abroad were ordinarily entertained there. And commoners of our own land who had attained prominence paced its Peacock Alley daily.

Yet the building in which all of these events centered has passed and a mightier skyscraper stands in its place, while in the newer residential district on fashionable Park Avenue another Waldorf-Astoria has reared its twin towers into the skyline. All this seems the more remarkable when one realizes that one hundred years ago the site of the original Waldorf building was a small field on one of the prettiest farms of Manhattan Island. A brook babbled across the property and an occasional wagon rumbled on the dusty Bloomingdale Road.

The roster of the old Bar's patrons would seem almost the record of a period in American life, J. Pierpont Morgan, the elder, used to call for a Manhattan cocktail after the market closed. Senator Marcus Alonzo Hanna, power behind the throne in the McKinley administration, called when in New York. Samuel Langhorne Clemens, better known as Mark Twain, was an occasional visitor, accompanied by his friend H. H. Rogers, of the Standard Oil Company.

Colonel William F. Cody, otherwise "Buffalo Bill"; Vice President Charles Warren Fairbanks; Senator Matthew Stanley Quay, the iron boss of Pennsylvania; Alfred E. Smith, Sheriff, Governor and candidate for the Presidency; John W. Gates, always ready to "bet you a million"; General Nelson A. Miles; Diamond Jim Brady; Richard Croker and Charley Murphy of Tammany Hall—there were always numerous celebrities at the Bar, or leaving, or shortly to come.

Actors rubbed elbows with financiers and athletes with industrial giants. Richard Harding Davis, author and war correspondent, came occasionally, as did John McGraw of the baseball fame. There were noted prize fighters—John L. Sullivan, Jim Jeffries, Tom Sharkey and "Gentleman Jim" Corbett. Many, including Nat Goodwin, Peter Dailey and W. H. Crane, represented the stage. Great publishers and editors, including Colonel ("Marse Henry") Watterson, visited the Waldorf Bar.

But a list of prominent patrons would read like many pages from "Who's Who in America" and space forbids. The point is that the Bar attracted these men of fastidious tastes because its drinks were what they ought to be. Numerous formulas were created there— to meet the challenges of guests.

A number of drinks dispensed at the Old Waldorf Bar and new drinks originated at the new Waldorf Bar— "Lounge Cafe", will be found on the following pages.

May they gladden many a heart!

ART OF MIXING DRINKS

MEASURES

One dash equals one-third teaspoonful

Jigger—a bartender's measure equivalent to one and one-half ounces (or small whiskey glass)

Pony—equals one ounce

Definition
    Frappe: fill cocktail glass three-quarters full shaved ice

COCKTAILS

(Serve in cocktail glass unless otherwise specified)

ABSINTHE

Two dashes of Old Tom Gin
Two-thirds Absinthe
One-third Water
Ice, stir, strain

ADONIS

Two dashes Orange Bitters
One-half Sherry
One-half Italian Vermuth
Ice, stir, strain

ALEXANDER

One-third Old Tom Gin
One-third Creme de Cacao
One-third Cream
Frappé

ASTORIA

Two dashes Abbott's Orange Bitters
One-third Old Tom Gin
Two-thirds French Vermuth
Ice, stir, strain

BACARDI COCKTAIL

One-half pony Grenadine
Two-thirds jigger Bacardi Rum
Juice of one-half Lemon
Ice, shake well

BIJOU

Two dashes Abbott's Bitters
One-half French Vermuth
One-half Grand Marnier
Ice, stir, strain

BIRD

Twist two pieces Orange Peel
Fill glass with fine ice
Two-thirds Triple Sec Curacao
One-third Martell Brandy
Two more twisted Orange Peels
Serve as Cremé de Menthe Frappé

BLUE MOON

One-fourth Creme Yvette
Three-fourths Old Tom Gin
Ice, shake

BRANDY

One dash Abbott's Bitters
One dash Dry Gin
One jigger Martell's Brandy
Ice, stir

BRIDAL

Two dashes Orange Bitters
Dash of maraschino
One-third jigger Italian Vermuth
Two-thirds Plymouth Gin
Ice, stir, strain
One piece Orange Peel, twisted

BRONX

    One-fourth French Vermuth
    One-fourth Italian Vermuth
    One-half High & Dry Gin
    One-fourth slice Orange
    Ice, shake well

CHAMPAGNE

    (Champagne glass)
    One lump sugar
    Two dashes Abbott's Bitters
    One piece Lemon Peel, twisted in glass
    Lump of ice, Dry Monopole Champagne

CHARLIE CHAPLIN

    One-third Lime Juice
    One-third Field's Sloe Gin
    One-third Apricot Brandy
    Ice, shake

CLOVER CLUB

    Juice of one-half Lemon
    White of one egg
    One jigger House of Lords Gin
    One bar-spoon Grenadine
    Ice, shake

CLOVER LEAF

    Juice of one-half Lemon
    White of one egg
    One jigger Old Tom Gin
    One bar-spoonful sugar
    Ice, shake well, strain in original Claret glass, place one sprig of mint on top of drink

CREOLE

Dash of Orange Bitters
One-third jigger Absinthe
One-third jigger Italian Vermuth
One-third jigger Old Tom Gin
Frappe

DAIQUIRI

One-third jigger Lime Juice
Two-thirds jigger Bacardi Rum
One bar-spoonful sugar
Ice, shake well, strain

DUBONNET COCKTAIL

One-half Dubonnet
One-half High & Dry Gin
Ice, shake well

FULL HOUSE

Dash of Abbott's Bitters
One-third Yellow Chartreuse
One-third Benedictine
One-third Apple Whiskey
Frappe

GIN

Dash of Orange Bitters
One jigger Old Tom Gin
Ice, stir, strain

GOAT'S DELIGHT

      One-half Kirschwasser
      One-half Brandy
      One dash Orgeat or Orange Syrup
      One spoon Cream
      One dash Absinthe
      Frappe

GOOD TIMES

      Dash of Orange Bitters
      One-third French Vermuth
      Two-thirds Booth's Gin
      Ice, stir, strain
      Olive

HAPPY DAYS

      Dash of Orange Bitters
      One-eighth Italian Vermuth
      One-eighth French Vermuth
      Three-fourths Old Tom Gin
      Ice, stir, strain

HONOLULU

      Two dashes Abbott's Bitters
      One teaspoon Lime Juice
      One teaspoon Orange Juice
      One jigger Old Tom Gin
      Frappe, twist Lemon Peel on top

HOP FROG

      One-third Lime Juice
      Two-thirds Brandy
      Frappe

JACK ROSE

(Serve in Delmonico glass)
One jigger Apple Jack
Juice one-half Lime
One-half jigger Grenadine
Shake well

MANHATTAN

One dash Angostura Bitters
One-third jigger Italian Vermuth
Two-thirds jigger Rye Whiskey
One lump ice, stir or shake as requested
One cherry

MARTELL COCKTAIL

Juice of one-half fresh Lime
One-half teaspoon strained honey
One jigger Brandy
Mix lime juice with honey, add Brandy, ice, shake well
Serve in cocktail glass with thin slice of lemon and one maraschino cherry

MARTINI

Dash of Orange Bitters
One-half Old Tom Gin
One-half Italian Vermuth
Ice, stir, strain

MARTINI DRY

One-third jigger French Vermuth
Two-thirds jigger Dry Gin
Stir, add small, green olive

MAE WEST

    One jigger Martell Brandy
    One dash Grenadine
    Juice of one-half Lime
    Ice, shake, strain
    Two Cherries in cocktail glass

MERRY WIDOW

    One-half French Vermuth
    One-half Dubonnet
    Frappe
    Green Cherry

MONOPOLE COCKTAIL

    (Serve in champagne glass)
    One-half lump of sugar
    One dash Abbott's Bitters
    Strip Orange Peel—twisted
    Lump of ice
    Fill with Champagne

NEW WALDORF

    One-fourth slice pineapple, crushed
    One-fourth French Vermuth
    One-fourth Italian Vermuth
    One-half House of Lords Gin
    Ice, shake well, strain

OLD FASHIONED

    One lump sugar
    One dash Abbott's Bitters
    One jigger Rye Whiskey
    One-half slice orange, one cherry
    Stick Pineapple
    Dash of syphon, lump of ice
    Serve in old fashioned glass

ORANGE BLOSSOM

> One-half jigger Orange Juice
> One-half jigger Old Tom Gin
> Ice, shake well

PEACOCK ALLEY

> Juice one-half Lime
> One-third Maple Syrup
> Two-thirds Charleston Rum
> Ice, shake well, strain

PEACOCK GALLERY

> Two dashes Abbott's Bitters
> One dash Absinthe
> One jigger Cordon Bleu Brandy
> Frappé

PEG O' MY HEART

> One half Lime Juice
> One-half Bacardi Rum
> Color with Grenadine
> Frappé

PICK ME UP

> Two dashes Acid or Lemon Phosphate
> One-half Italian Vermuth
> One-half Absinthe
> Ice, shake, strain

POET'S DREAM

    One-third Benedictine
    One-third French Vermuth
    One-third High & Dry Gin
    Ice, shake, Lemon Peel, squeezed on top

ROB ROY

    One-half jigger Italian Vermuth
    One-half jigger Vat 69 Scotch Whiskey
    One dash Orange Bitters
    Ice, shake well

RUSSIAN GRAND DUKE

    Two-thirds Cordon Bleu Brandy
    One-third Orange Juice
    Dash of Orange Bitters
    Dash of Absinthe
    Ice, shake well

SALOME

    Two dashes Absinthe
    One half Italian Vermuth
    One-half Dubonnet
    Ice, stir, strain

SEPTEMBER MORN

    Juice of one Lime
    One jigger of Bacardi Rum
    White of one egg
    Color with Grenadine
    Frappe well; serve in Claret glass

SHERRY-NETHERLAND

    Dash of Orange Bitters
    Two-thirds Martell Brandy
    One-third Curacao
    Ice, stir, strain

SIDE CAR

Juice of one-half Lime
One-third Cointreau
Two-thirds Martell Brandy
Ice, shake

SLOE GIN

Dash of Orange Bitters
Two-thirds Field's Sloe Gin
One-third Plymouth Gin
Ice, stir, strain

SOUL KISS

(Delmonico glass)
One-third French Vermuth
Two-thirds Dry Gin
White of one egg, Cherry, Frappe

SOURS

WHISKEY
BRANDY
SCOTCH
GIN
BOURBON
APPLE JACK

(Delmonico glass)
One jigger liquor desired
Juice one-half lemon
One teaspoon sugar
Ice, stir, strain
Fill with syphon
One-half slice orange

TODDIES

WHISKEY
BRANDY
SCOTCH

(Old fashioned glass)
One jigger liquor desired
One-half lump sugar
Three teaspoons water
Lump of ice, stir
One-half slice orange, one cherry, lemon peel

TOM GIN

Dash of Orange Bitters
One jigger Old Tom Gin
Ice, stir, strain

TRILBY

Dash of Orange Bitters
One-third French Vermuth
Two-thirds Old Tom Gin
One dash of Creme Yvette
Ice, stir, strain

WALDORF

Dash of Abbott's Bitters
One-third Whiskey
One-third Absinthe
One-third Italian Vermuth
Frappe

WALDORF GLOOM LIFTER

Made same as Clover Club, but use Irish Whiskey
One-half teaspoon Martell Brandy
White of one egg
Dash of Raspberry Syrup
Dash of Grenadine
One-half teaspoon sugar
Ice, stir, strain

WALDORF-ASTORIA

Pony of Benedictine on shaved ice
Cover and build in mound with sweetened whipped cream

WHISKEY SOUR

(Delmonico glass)
One-half Lemon Juice
One jigger Rye Whiskey
One bar-spoonful sugar
Ice, shake, fill with syphon
One-half slice of Orange

ZAZA

One-half jigger High & Dry Gin
One-half jigger Dubonnet
Ice, shake well

BABY TITTY
(Sherry glass)
One-third Anisette
One-third Creme Yvette
One-third Whipped Cream
Serve with cherry on top

BRANDY AND GINGER ALE FRAPPE
Tom Collins glass
One jigger Martell Brandy
Fill with fine ice
Shake well, strain, fill with cold ginger ale

BRANDY FIZZ
(Lemonade glass)
One jigger Martell Brandy
Juice one-half lemon
One teaspoon sugar
Ice, shake, strain
Fill with syphon

BRANDY FLOAT
Pony of Brandy, floated on seltzer in whiskey glass

BRANDY JULEP
Put three of four sprigs of Mint in mixing glass
One-half spoon sugar
One pony of water
Crush well, fill two-thirds goblet with ice
One jigger Martell's Brandy
Fruit well, decorate with sprigs of Mint

BRANDY PUNCH
(Goblet)
Juice of one-half Lemon
One-half spoonful sugar
One pony of water
One jigger Brandy
Ice, shake, strain, fruit goblet

BRANDY SMASH

    (Fizz glass)
    Two sprigs Mint
    Two spoons water
    One-quarter spoon sugar
    Muddle
    One jigger Brandy
    Two lumps ice
    Small spoon

BRANDY TODDY

    (Old fashioned glass)
    One-half lump sugar
    Three spoons water
    One jigger Brandy
    One lump ice
    Small spoon
    One-half slice Orange, one Cherry, Lemon Peel

CHAMPAGNE CUP

    (Pitcher)
    One and one-half ponies Martell Brandy
    One pony Benedictine
    One pony Maraschino
    One bottle Soda
    One bottle Dry Monopole Champagne
    One stick ice
    Fruit, decorate with Mint

CHAMPAGNE PUNCH

    (Pitcher)
    One pint Champagne
    One pint Claret or Red Burgundy
    One pint Club Soda
    One sliced Orange—Two lumps sugar—Ice
    Fruit in season

CLARET CUP WALDORF
(Pitcher)
In mixing glass, put
One-half spoon sugar
One and one-half ponies Brandy
One pony Benedictine
One pony Maraschino
Seltzer to fill glass
Stir, pour into pitcher, add large stick ice
One bottle Claret
Fruit, decorate with frosted Mint

CLARET LEMONADE
Lemonade with dash of Claret

CLARET PUNCH
One jigger Claret
Four dashes Lemon
Two dashes Curacao
Two dishes Grenadine
Goblet glass, fine ice dressed with fruits in season

CLARET PUNCH
(Two quarts)
Juice three Lemons
One pony Curacao
One pony Brandy
One-half tablespoon sugar
One quart Claret
One syphon
Ice, dress with fruit in season

EGG NOGGS

BRANDY RUM SCOTCH SHERRY RYE	(Lemonade glass) One jigger liquor desired One-half spoon sugar One egg Fill three-quarters with Milk Ice, shake well, strain, Nutmeg on top

FASCINATION
(Champagne glass)
One-third White Curacao
Two-thirds White Absinthe
One piece of ice in glass
Fill from syphon

FISH HOUSE PUNCH
(Delmonico glass)
Juice one-half Lemon
One-half spoon sugar
One-half jigger Brandy
One-half Jamaica Rum
Ice, shake well, fruit in season

FLIPS
BRANDY
WHISKEY
PORT
SHERRY

(Delmonico glass)
One jigger liquor desired
Whole egg
One teaspoon sugar
Ice, shake and strain
Nutmeg on top

FLORADORA SEXTETTE
(Collins glass)
Juice one Lime
One-half teaspoon sugar
One-half pony Raspberry
One jigger High & Dry Gin
Frappé, fizz with one bottle ginger ale

GIN BUCK
(Collins)
One drink of Old Tom Gin
Juice of one Lemon
One lump ice
One bottle Ginger Ale

GIN DAISY
(Goblet glass)
Juice of one-half Lemon
One jigger Gin
One-half jigger Grenadine
Fine ice and fruits in season

GIN FIZZ
(Fizz glass)
Juice of one-half Lemon
One bar-spoonful sugar
One jigger Gin
Ice, shake, strain, fill with syphon

GOLDEN FIZZ
(Lemonade glass)
Juice one-half Lemon
Bar-spoonful sugar
Yoke of one egg
One jigger Gin
Ice, shake, strain, fill with syphon

GOLDEN WEST
(Sherry glass)
One-quarter Yellow Chartreuse
White of one egg
Fill with Sherry

GRENADINE FIZZ
(Lemonade glass)
Juice of one-half Lemon
One-half spoon sugar
One pony Grenadine
One pony Milk
One jigger Old Tom Gin
Ice, shake, strain, fill from syphon

HIGHBALLS
SCOTCH WHISKEY
RYE
BOURBON
GIN
BRANDY

(Eight or twelve ounce Highball glass)
One jigger liquor desired
Lump of ice
Fill with Club Soda or Gingerale, according to taste

HONEYMOON
(Sherry glass)
One-third Crême de Cacao
One-third Parfait d'Amour
Yolk of one egg
One-third Kummel Doré

HORSES NECK
(Tom Collins glass)
Rind of one Lemon
One bottle Ginger Ale

JOHN COLLINS
(Tom Collins glass)
Juice whole lemon
One jigger gin
One teaspoon powdered sugar
Ice, shake, strain
Fill with Club Soda

LALLA ROOKH
(Lemonade)
One pony Vanilla
One-half jigger Martell Brandy
One-half Jamaica Rum
One-half spoon sugar
One tablespoon whipped cream
Ice, shake well, strain

MINT COOLER
(Collins)
Three or four sprigs of Mint
Two lumps of ice
One bottle Ginger Ale

MINT JULEP
    (Tom Collins glass)
    One bar-spoonful sugar
    Four sprigs fresh Mint, one-half pony water, press well
    Add one jigger Bourbon Whiskey
    Stir, fill glass with fine ice to frost, fruit in season, place bunch mint on top and serve with straws

MORNING GLORY FIZZ
    (Fizz glass)
    Juice one-half Lemon
    One-half spoon sugar
    White of one egg
    One jigger Sanderson's Scotch
    Two dashes Absinthe
    Shake, strain, fill from syphon

NEW ORLEANS FIZZ
    (Lemonade glass)
    Juice of one-half Lemon
    Two dashes Orange Flower water
    One spoonful sugar
    One jigger Cream
    White of one egg
    One jigger of Gin
    Shake *well*, strain, add a little syphon

ORANGE COGNAC
    Cut orange in half, remove pulp,
      , turn inside out, place rind in glass
    Fill with shaved ice
    Pour over it Martell Cognac

POUSSE CAFE WALDORF
    (Sherry glass)
    One-seventh Raspberry Syrup
    One-seventh Anisette
    One-seventh Parfait d'Amour
    One-seventh Créme Yvette
    One-seventh Yellow Chartreuse
    One-seventh Green Chartreuse
    One-seventh Cordon Bleu Brandy

REMSEN COOLER
    (Lemonade)
    Juice of one-half Lime
    Lemon rind
    One jigger Gin, ice
    One bottle Club Soda

RICKEYS
SLOE GIN
GIN
BRANDY
WHISKEY

    (Eight ounce Highball glass)
    One jigger liquor desired
    Juice one-half lime
    Ice
    Fill with Club Soda

ROOSEVELT PUNCH
    (Goblet)
    Muddle one-half Lemon
    One spoon sugar
    One jigger Apple Whiskey
    Shake, one dash of Brandy on top
    Fruit in season

ROYAL FIZZ
    (Lemonade glass)
    Juice of one-half Lemon
    One bar-spoonful sugar
    One whole egg
    One jigger Gin
    Shake, strain, fill with syphon

SHERRY COBLER
    One bar-spoonful sugar
    One jigger Sherry
    One-half Lemon Juice
    Serve with goblet filled with ice and dress with fruits in season, fill with syphon

SILVER FIZZ
(Fizz glass)
Juice of one-half Lemon
One bar-spoonful sugar
White of one egg
One jigger Gin
Ice, shake, strain, fill with syphon

SLOE GIN FIZZ
(Fizz glass)
Juice of one-half Lemon
One spoonful sugar
One jigger Field's Sloe Gin
Ice, shake, strain, fill with syphon

SNOWBALL
(Collins)
White of one egg
One jigger Charleston Rum
One-half spoon sugar
Ice, shake, strain, fill with Ginger Ale

STARLIGHT ROOF GARDEN COOLER
(Collins glass)
Juice of one Lime
One dash Bitters on one lump sugar
One jigger French Vermouth
One bottle of Ginger Ale, ice

TOM AND JERRY
(Beer mug)
Beat six eggs well, adding powdered sugar until very thick, working out all lumps
Pour one-half tablespoon of this batter into mug
One-half jigger Brandy
One-half jigger Jamaica Rum
Fill with very hot water
Add Nutmeg
Serve with napkin

TOM COLLINS

(Collins glass)
Juice of one Lemon
One spoonful powdered sugar
One jigger Old Tom Gin
Tom Collins glass, with ice
Mix well and strain in glass with
One bottle of Club Soda

WALDORF FIZZ

(Lemonade glass)
Juice of one Orange
Juice of one Lemon
One jigger High & Dry Gin
One egg
One spoonful sugar
Ice, shake, strain, fill glass with syphon

WHISKEY AND MINT

(Whiskey glass)
Three springs Mint
One-half lump sugar, dissolved, press Mint lightly
One jigger Rye Whiskey
Small lump of ice

WHISKEY DAISY

(Fizz)
Juice of one-half Lemon
One-half spoon sugar
One pony Raspberry Syrup
One jigger Whiskey
Ice, shake, strain, fill with syphon

WHISKEY FIZZ

      (Lemonade glass)
      One-half spoon sugar
      One-half pony of water
      Three or four lumps of ice
      One jigger Whiskey
      Ice, one-half slice orange, one-half slice lemon
      Serve with spoon

WHISKEY MINT JULEP

      (Goblet)
      Three sprigs Mint
      One-half spoon sugar
      One pony of water
      Press well, add one jigger Bourbon Whiskey
      Stir, strain well, fruit in season

WHISKEY PUNCH

      (Goblet)
      Juice of one-half Lemon
      One-half spoon sugar
      One pony of water
      Fill glass two-thirds with fine ice
      One jigger Whiskey
      Stir, fruit well in season

WHISKEY SMASH

      (Fizz)
      Three sprigs of Mint
      Fill with fine ice in mixing glass
      Two more sprigs of Mint
      One-quarter spoon sugar
      One-half pony of water
      Press well and add one jigger Whiskey
      Stir, strain, fruit well, Mint on top

CORDIALS

ANGEL'S BLUSH OR KISS
>(Pony)
>Two-thirds Benedictine
>One-third Cream

ANGEL'S DREAM
>(Pony)
>One-third Maraschino
>One-third Cream
>One-third Creme Yvette

BRANDY SCAFFA
>(Pony)
>One-half Maraschino
>One-half Martell Brandy
>Two dashes Angostura on top

COME UP—SOME TIME
>(Cordial glass)
>One-third Brizzard Apricot Brandy
>One-third Martell Brandy
>Float one-third cream on top
>Top with Maraschino Cherry

www.ingramcontent.com/pod-product-compliance
Lightning Source LLC
Chambersburg PA
CBHW060543080526
44586CB00012B/841